Contents

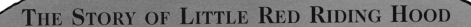

THE STORY OF LITTLE RED RIDING HOOD

When Red Riding Hood walks through the forest to her Grandma's house she meets a wicked Wolf who soon gets up to no good. Don't worry, though. Like all good fairytales there is a happy ending.

Choose a Part

This play is a story that you can read with your friends and perhaps even act out in front of an audience. You need up to five people. Before you start, choose which parts you would like to play.

These two parts can be played by one person.

Wicked Wolf
A greedy mean wolf who likes to eat people.

Grandma
A sweet old lady, who could be a wolf!

Red Riding Hood
A kind little girl.

Woodcutter
He appears at the end to save everyone.

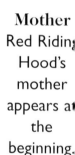

Mother
Red Riding Hood's mother appears at the beginning.

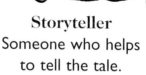

Storyteller
Someone who helps to tell the tale.

How many people are going to take part?

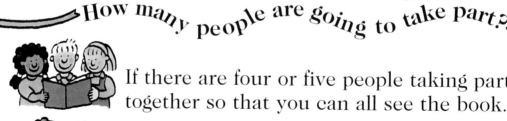

If there are four or five people taking part, sit together so that you can all see the book.

If there are two or three people, share out the parts between you.

If you want to read the play on your own, use a different sounding voice for each part.

PLAYTALES

LITTLE RED RIDING HOOD

MOIRA BUTTERFIELD

Heinemann

First published in Great Britain in 1997 by Heinemann Children's Reference,
an imprint of Heinemann Educational Publishers,
Halley Court, Jordan Hill, Oxford, OX2 8EJ,
a division of Reed Educational & Professional Publishing Ltd.

MADRID ATHENS PRAGUE WARSAW FLORENCE PORTSMOUTH NH
CHICAGO SAO PAULO SINGAPORE TOKYO MEXICO MELBOURNE
AUCKLAND IBADAN GABORONE JOHANNESBURG KAMPALA NAIROBI

ISBN 0 431 08143 3 Hb   ISBN 0 431 08148 4 Pb

A CIP catalogue record for this book is available at the British Library.

Co-author: Robin Edwards
Editor: David Riley
Art Director: Cathy Tincknell
Designer: Anne Sharples
Photography: Trever Clifford
Illustrator: Frances Cony
Props: Anne Sharples

Thanks to: Carlie Townsend, Amy Livesey,
George Suttie and Shaka Omwony

Printed and bound in Italy.

You will need to use scissors and glue to
make the props for your play. Always
make sure an adult is there to help you.

Use only water-based face paints and
make-up. Children with sensitive skin
should use make-up and face paints
with caution.

Reading the Play

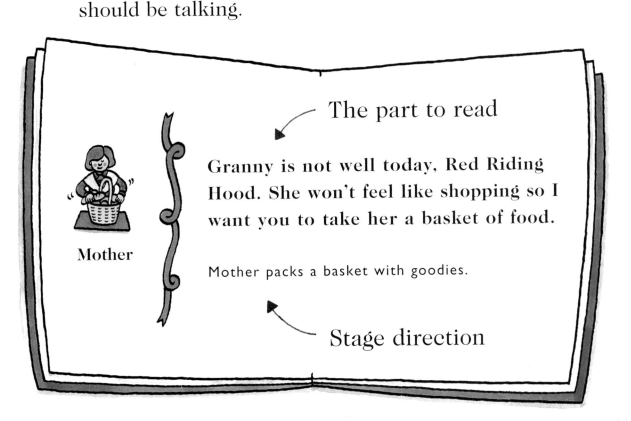

Red Riding Hood   Wolf   Grandma   Mother   Woodcutter   Storyteller

The play is made up of different parts. Next to each part there is a name and a picture. This shows who should be talking.

The part to read

Mother

Granny is not well today, Red Riding Hood. She won't feel like shopping so I want you to take her a basket of food.

Mother packs a basket with goodies.

Stage direction

In between the parts there are some stage directions. They are suggestions for things you might do, such as making a noise or miming an action.

5

Things to Make

Here are some suggestions for dressing the part.

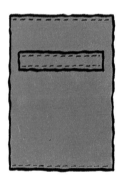

RED RIDING HOOD: CLOTHES AND PROPS

Wear a dress and carry a basket of food (borrow some bits and pieces from the kitchen). If you haven't got a basket a carrier bag will do.

Make a Cloak

You need:

- A piece of red fabric 1m square or more
- A strip of fabric 80mm by 950mm
- Scissors, pencil and ruler
- A strip of ribbon about 750mm long
- A needle and thread or glue

1. Lay the fabric out. Glue or sew a hem along the top and bottom edges.

2. Sew or glue a strip of fabric 350mm from the top edge to make a 'channel'. Thread the ribbon through.

3. Wrap the cloak around your shoulders, and tie the ribbon. Pull the large collar over your head to make a hood.

If you don't want to make a cloak, just wear a red scarf or a red coat with a hood.

Facepainting Ideas

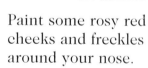

Paint some rosy red cheeks and freckles around your nose.

WOLF: CLOTHES AND PROPS

Wear a grey t-shirt with a belt tied round your waist, and grey leggings or trousers.

Make a Tail

You need:
- Scissors
- Three strips of grey fabric or pieces cut from a grey bin liner, 500mm by 80mm

1. Snip the bottom edge of each strip to make a fringe. Knot the strips together above the fringes.

2. Wind the strips round and round each other.

3. Then knot them together near the top. Now tuck your tail into the back of your belt.

Make a Wolf Mask

You need:
- Some scrap paper and a strip of card 250mm by 200mm
- Scissors and pencil
- Strip of elastic and glue

Make a mask out of scrap paper first, to make sure it fits you. Then copy the size onto the card.

1. Cut the shape of the wolf head and ears out of the card.

2. Cut the eye holes out of the mask and decorate it. Stick the ears on, and thread the elastic at each side to go around the back of your head.

Grandma Disguise

Slip an old dressing gown on to become Grandma.

Make a pair of glasses from five pipe cleaners.

Fold an old scarf into a triangle and cut two slits to fit your ears through.

If you are playing Grandma as well as the Wolf, don't paint your face because you will need to appear as both characters.

Facepainting Ideas

Paint the end of your nose black and add a black line between your nose and mouth. Put small black dots on your 'muzzle'.

MOTHER: CLOTHES AND PROPS

Wear a dress and a scarf around your neck. Add a necklace to make you look more grown-up.

WOODCUTTER: CLOTHES AND PROPS

Wear a baseball cap, jeans and a shirt. Wear a large belt and carry an axe.

Make an Axe

You need:
- A long cardboard tube from the middle of a kitchen foil or wrapping roll
- Some thin card (an empty cereal packet will do)
- Tape measure
- Glue
- Paint
- Scissors

1. Cut a piece of card as shown, with an axe-shape at either end and a thinner strip in the middle.

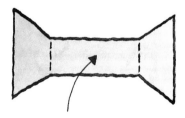

This strip should be long enough to fit round your tube. Measure it with a tape measure.

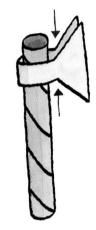

2. Glue the strip around the top of the tube and glue the axe heads together.

3. Once the glue is dry paint your axe any colour you like.

Facepainting Ideas for Mother

Make your cheeks rosy and wear some pretty lipstick.

Stage and Sounds

Once you have read the play through you may want to perform it in front of an audience. If so, read through this section first. It has been kept very simple, and you may want to add some extra performance ideas of your own in rehearsal.

COSTUME CHANGES

People who play more than one part will occasionally need to change costume. The stage directions tell you when to do this. Keep your costumes off-stage and out of sight, perhaps behind a table covered with a tablecloth or on a table hidden behind an open door.

REHEARSING

Rehearse the play before you ask someone to watch.

PROPS

Position a chair on stage. You will need this to represent Grandma's bed. If you like, cover your legs with a blanket.

Keep any other props out of sight of the audience.

SOUNDS

Knocking on Grandma's door: Knock a knuckle on the back of your book or on a nearby chair.

Fighting:

Go off-stage when the Wolf eats Grandma and later fights with the Woodcutter, so the audience can't see you. Then make shouting and scuffling noises as if you are fighting.

The Play

Storyteller

Once upon a time there was a little girl called Red Riding Hood. She got her name because she wore a red cloak with a hood to keep herself warm in winter.

The Storyteller points to Little Red Riding Hood and then to her Mother.

Storyteller

Red Riding Hood lived with her Mother on the edge of a thick forest. Her Grandmother lived on the other side of the wood at the end of a long winding path. One day Grandma fell ill...

Mother

Granny is not well today, Red Riding Hood. She won't feel like shopping so I want you to take her a basket of food.

Mother packs a basket with goodies.

Red Riding Hood

Poor Granny. I'll do my best to cheer her up.

Storyteller

Red Riding Hood's mother hands her the basket of tasty food. She waves goodbye and gives a warning...

Mother hands Red Riding Hood the basket. They wave to each other.

Mother

Stay on the path and don't talk to strangers, especially not wolves. Remember, never trust a Wolf!

Red Riding Hood sings softly as she carries the basket.

Red Riding Hood

> Tra la, la, la. What a lovely sunny day it is. What a pity poor Granny is too ill to get out of bed and enjoy the sunshine.

The Wolf pops up behind Red Riding Hood and whispers to himself.

Wolf

> Ho, ho! Old Granny's stuck in bed, eh? I think I'll pay her a visit just in time for lunch.

Storyteller

The Wolf scampers off towards Grandma's cottage, chuckling softly to himself.

The Wolf chuckles. The noise makes Red Riding Hood jump.

Red Riding Hood

What was that? It must have been a bunny...

Storyteller

A bunny? Oh, dear me no. It wasn't a bunny. It was the wicked Wolf himself! Be careful Red Riding Hood!

Someone needs to do Grandma's voice here, though the audience don't need to see her. One of the other players could do it off-stage.

Start by making a knocking noise (do it on the back of your book).

Grandma

Who is it?

Wolf
(pretending to be Red Riding Hood)

It's me,
Red Riding Hood.

Grandma

Oh, how lovely.
Come in dear.
The door's open.

COSTUME CHANGE

The person playing the Wolf runs out of sight and pretends to have a fight, making shrieking and thumping noises. Then the Wolf comes back licking his lips, wearing the granny glasses, dressing gown and scarf over his ears (see page 7).

Wolf

Yum, yum! That Granny was delicious! My second course will be coming along in a minute.

If you wish, the Wolf can sit on a chair to represent Grandma's bed. His knees could be covered with a blanket. There is another knock on the door.

Red Riding Hood

Granny, it's Red Riding Hood.

Wolf
(whispers to himself)

Oh, good. Here comes the rest of my meal!

Wolf
(pretending to be Grandma)

Come in, dear. The door's open.

Red Riding Hood

Hello, Granny. My, you do look ill. I've brought you a basket of food to make you feel a little better.

Wolf
(pretending to be Grandma)

How kind. Come a little closer so I can see you...

Red Riding Hood puts her basket down and peers at the Wolf dressed as Grandma.

Ooh, Granny. What big eyes you have!

Red Riding Hood

All the better to see you with, my dear! Come a little closer.

Wolf
(pretending to be Grandma)

My, what big ears you have!

Red Riding
Hood

All the better to hear you with, my dear!
Now come a little closer.

Wolf
(pretending
to be
Grandma)

20

Red Riding Hood

Oh my, oh my. What big teeth you have!

Wolf

All the better to EAT you with, girlie!

The Wolf chases Red Riding Hood around.

Wolf

Come here, little girl!
I'm still hungry!

Red Riding Hood

Help, help!

Storyteller

Poor Red Riding Hood is about to become a Wolf snack. Then suddenly the door bursts open and in strides the Woodcutter, carrying his axe.

Woodcutter

What's all the noise? Ah ha! So it's you, you rotten Wolf! Right, I'll fix you, my furry friend.

The Woodcutter chases the Wolf around with his axe.

"Help, help!"

Wolf

COSTUME CHANGE

The Wolf and the Woodcutter run out of sight but you can still hear them shrieking and pretending to fight. While off-stage the person playing the Wolf takes off the wolf mask and gives it to the Woodcutter.

Woodcutter
(off-stage)

> Chop, chop! We'll have no more trouble from you, Mr Wolf! Now then ... let's see... Chop, chop. Ah, I thought as much! Out you come, Granny!

The Woodcutter appears carrying the wolf mask.

Red Riding Hood

Oh thank you, Mr Woodcutter!

Red Riding Hood hugs the Woodcutter.

Woodcutter

The wicked Wolf is dead.

The Woodcutter holds up the wolf mask.

Storyteller

And so our story ended happily. Grandma was saved from the Wolf's tummy. Red Riding Hood got safely home and the woods were not troubled by wolves again.

If you like, finish the play with a loud wolf howl!